Master Math

GET TO KNOW NUMBERS

Numbers up to 100 and place value

ANJANA CHATTERJEE   ILLUSTRATED BY JO SAMWAYS

CONSULTATION BY
RUTH BULL, BSc (HONS), PGCE, MA (ED)

Quarto is the authority on a wide range of topics.

Quarto educates, entertains and enriches the lives of our readers—enthusiasts and lovers of hands-on living.

www.quartoknows.com

Author: Anjana Chatterjee
Consultant: Ruth Bull, BSc (HONS), PGCE, MA (ED)
Designers: emojo design and Victoria Kimonidou
Illustrator: Jo Samways
Editors: Claire Watts and Ellie Brough

© 2018 Quarto Publishing plc
First Published in 2018 by The Quarto Library,
an imprint of The Quarto Group.
6 Orchard Road, Suite 100
Lake Forest, CA 92630
T: +1 949 380 7510
F: +1 949 380 7575
www.QuartoKnows.com

Distributed in the United States and Canada by
Lerner Publisher Services
241 First Avenue North
Minneapolis, MN 55401 U.S.A.
www.lernerbooks.com

A CIP record for this book is available at the Library of Congress.

ISBN 978 1 68297 319 6

9 8 7 6 5 4 3 2 1

Manufactured in DongGuan, China TL102017

MIX
Paper from
responsible sources
FSC® C104723

Hello, my name is Pango. I'm a pangolin and I love math! I'll be your guide to becoming a math master!

CONTENTS

Unit 1 Numbers 1 to 10 .... page 4

Unit 2 Number bonds .... page 14

Unit 3 Addition within 10 .... page 18

Unit 4 Subtraction within 10 .... page 22

Unit 5 Ordinal numbers .... page 26

Unit 6 Numbers to 100 .... page 28

Tools for success .... page 32

HOW TO USE THE BOOKS IN THIS SERIES

The four books in Year 1 of the Master Math series focus on the main strands of the curriculum but using the leading Singapore math approach. This method involves teaching children to think and explain mathematically, with an emphasis on problem solving, focusing on the following three-step approach:

1 Concrete

Children engage in hands-on learning activities using concrete objects such as counters, cubes, dice, paper clips, or buttons. For example, children might add 4 cubes and 3 cubes together.

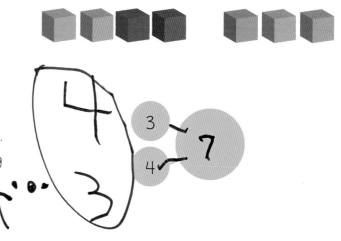

2 Pictorial

Children draw pictorial representations of mathematical concepts. For example, children might draw a number bond diagram showing that 3 and 4 together make 7.

3 Abstract

Children can then move on to solving mathematical problems in an abstract way by using numbers and symbols. Once children understand that 3 and 4 make 7 when they are added together, they can use the abstract method to record it.

$$3 + 4 = 7$$

Each unit of the book begins with a question or statement, which encourages children to begin thinking about a new mathematical concept. This is followed by visual explanations and hands-on activities that lead children to a deep conceptual understanding. Children should repeat and vary the activities, and be encouraged to revisit earlier sections to seek clarification and to deepen their understanding. You will find extension activities and further instruction in the Parent and Teacher Guidance sections.

Counting is lots of fun!

Let's learn how to **count** from 1 to 10.
Point your finger and count out loud.

1 one

2 two

3 three

4 four

5 five

6 six

7 seven

8 eight

9 nine

10 ten

TIME TO PRACTICE!

Look at the first row.
Can you see 1 orange?
Can you see 1 cube?

Count the number of each fruit
out loud and then count the cubes.

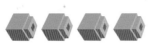

1 one

2 two

3 three

4 four

5 five

PARENT AND TEACHER GUIDANCE

- Counting out loud will help children to reinforce the number sequences and match numbers with number names.

- Call out any number between 1 and 10 and ask children to point to the correct number and its number name.

VOCABULARY: count

COUNT THE OBJECTS

These frames show numbers 6 to 10.
Count the objects in each frame.

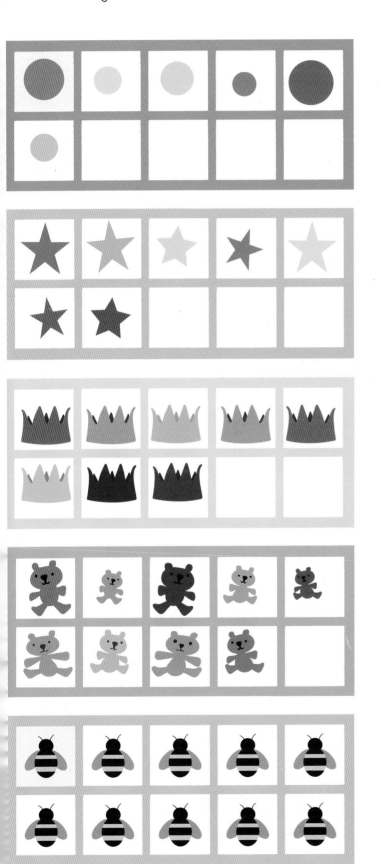

How many?

VOCABULARY: how many?

MAKE A COLORFUL NUMBER GARLAND

This number garland will help you learn numbers 1 to 10.

YOU WILL NEED:
- a round object to use as a template (for example, a cup)
- colored pencils
- colored cardstock
- scissors
- a hole punch
- string

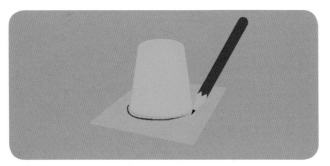

1 Draw around the cup ten times on the colored cardstock .

2 Ask an adult to help you carefully cut out the ten circles.

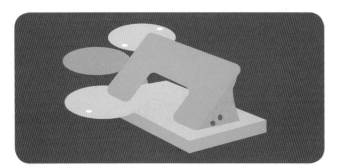

3 Punch two holes on each circle.

4 Use colored pencils to write numbers 1 to 10 in each circle.

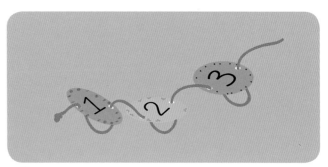

5 Thread the string down through one hole in each circle and up through the other.

6 Ask an adult to hang your number garland on the wall.

PARENT AND TEACHER GUIDANCE
- This activity will help to reinforce the sequence of the numbers in children's minds.

ZERO

Now let's look at the number **zero**.
Zero means nothing at all.

There are two apples
on the plate.

Sara and Liam eat
both apples.

There are no apples
on the plate.

There are zero apples.
We use the numeral **0** to show that there are no apples on the plate.

COUNTING DOWN

Look at the ducks on the pond.

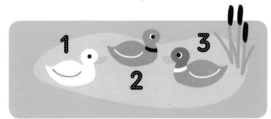

How many ducks are there?

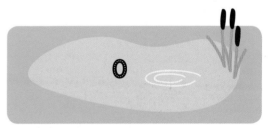

One duck flies away.
How many ducks now?

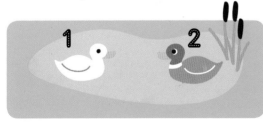

One duck flies away.
How many ducks now?

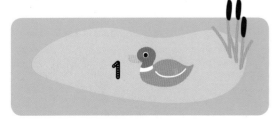

One duck flies away.
How many ducks now?

PARENT AND TEACHER GUIDANCE

• Repeat the counting down activity with cubes or everyday objects such as pencils, toys, or food items to show the concept of zero in real life.

• Count back from ten to zero using number rhymes or blasting off a toy rocket.

MATCHING NUMBERS

When numbers **match**, it means they are the **same**. Let's learn to match numbers.

Do these rows of cubes match?

5 cubes

5 cubes

same number of cubes

There are five cubes in the top row. There are five cubes in the bottom row. The number of cubes in both rows is the same. They are **equal**.

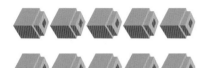

There are four hats.

There are four children.

The number of hats and the number of children is the same.
They are equal.

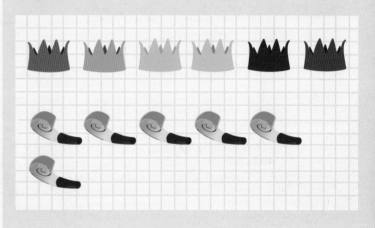

TRY THIS:
Look at the pictures below.
Are the numbers of the hats and whistles equal?

PARENT AND TEACHER GUIDANCE
- Set out a line of objects such as cubes or toys. Ask children to count the objects and make another line with the same number of objects.

- Ask them to explain what they are doing.

VOCABULARY: match, same, equal

COMPARING NUMBERS

When we **compare** numbers,
we see if the numbers match.

 5 cubes

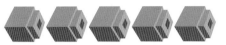 4 cubes

There are 5 cubes in the top row.
There are 4 cubes in the bottom row.
There are **more** cubes in the top row.
There are **fewer** cubes in the bottom row.

PARENT AND TEACHER GUIDANCE

- Ask children to make two sets of objects and compare them, such as toys or items of cutlery when setting the table.

- Encourage them to say which set has more and which has fewer.

- Ask for two sentences per activity.

There are four hats.

There are three children.

The number of hats and the number of children are not the same.
There are more hats than children.
There are fewer children than hats.

TRY THIS:

Compare the number of hats with the number of whistles. Write a sentence to describe the picture.

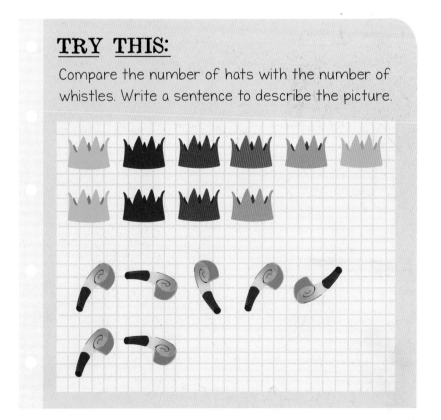

VOCABULARY: compare, more, fewer

These numbers are different. Let's count to find out how they are different.

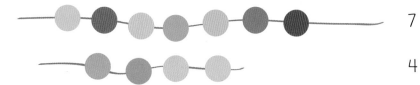

7

4

7 is more than 4.
4 is fewer than 7.

How many more?
Look at the line of 7 cubes.
Count along 4.

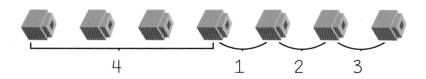

4   1   2   3

Now start counting again from 1 for the rest of the line.
7 is 3 more than 4.
4 is 3 fewer than 7.

TRY THIS:

Look at the pictures.

Which line has more?
Which line has fewer?
How many more?
How many fewer?

There are 2 more carrots than there are rabbits.
There are 2 fewer rabbits than there are carrots.

MORE OR FEWER

Look at the two sets of objects in each box.
Count and compare the numbers.

Which set has more objects?
Which set has fewer objects?

Which set has more objects?
Which set has fewer objects?

GREATER AND SMALLER

Count the flowers and the butterflies.

How many flowers are there?

There are eight flowers.

How many butterflies are there?

There are six butterflies.

There are more flowers than butterflies.
How do you know? Can you explain it?
8 is a **greater** number than 6.
A greater number is a number that is more.
6 is a **smaller** number than 8.
A smaller number is a number that is less.

Which number is greater?
5   or   **7**
7 is greater.

Which number is smaller?
9   or   **6**
6 is smaller.

VOCABULARY: greater, smaller

11

NUMBER LINE

We can use a **number line** to show all the numbers in order.

Look at the cars lining up at the traffic lights!

The red car is **before** the blue car.
Before means that it comes in front of the blue car.

The yellow car is **after** the blue car.
After means that it comes behind the blue car.

The blue car is **between** the yellow car and the red car.
Between means that it comes in the middle of the other two cars.

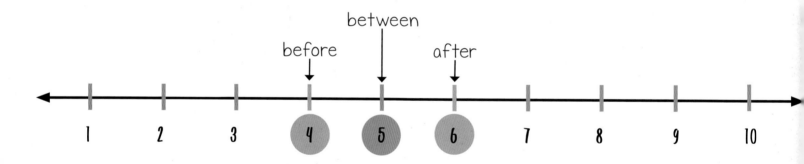

Look at the number 5 on the number line.

Which number comes before it?
4 comes before 5.

Which number comes after it?
6 comes after 5.

5 is between 4 and 6.

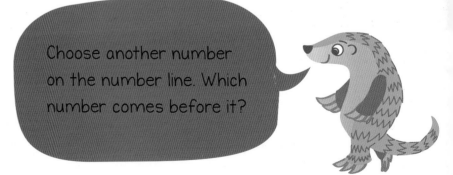

Choose another number on the number line. Which number comes before it?

VOCABULARY: number line, before, after, between

NUMBER PATTERNS

Can you make patterns with numbers?

A **pattern** is when things are arranged in a way that follows a rule.

Look at the patterns that the numbers make below. They are arranged from **smallest** to **greatest**.

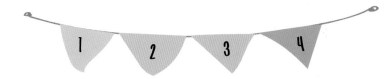

1 is smaller than 2.   2 is smaller than 3.   3 is smaller than 4.

The numbers below are arranged from greatest to smallest.

10 is greater than 9.   9 is greater than 8.   8 is greater than 7.

How many buttons should the last snowman have?

Each snowman in the pattern has 1 more button.
The last one should have 7 buttons.

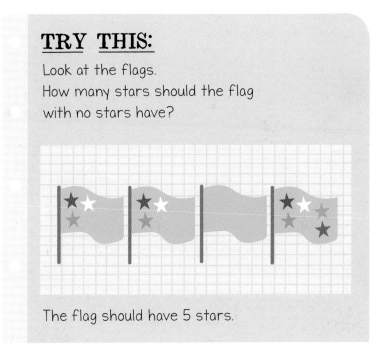

TRY THIS:

Look at the flags.
How many stars should the flag with no stars have?

The flag should have 5 stars.

PARENT AND TEACHER GUIDANCE

• Make sequences of number cards or quantities of objects to count. Ask children to say which numbers come before, after, or between different numbers. Have them continue number sequences or find a missing number in a sequence.

VOCABULARY: pattern, smallest, greatest

Let's look at how numbers join together to make other numbers.

Look at the picture below.

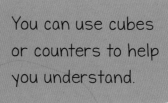

You can use cubes or counters to help you understand.

PARENT AND TEACHER GUIDANCE

● Expressing what number facts look like in a visual way will help children to see how numbers work. Whole numbers are made up of parts. If children know the parts, they will know how to put them together to find the whole. Start out working with smaller numbers and gradually work toward larger ones, and give children lots of practice with cubes and counters.

How many butterflies are by the pink flower?
How many butterflies are by the orange flower?
How many butterflies are there **altogether**?
There are 8 butterflies altogether.

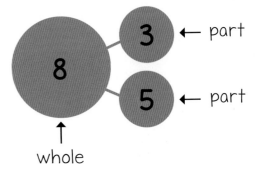

← part

← part

↑
whole

8 → 5 ← part
  → 3 ← part
↑
whole   5 and 3 make 8.

8 → 5 ← part
  → 3 ← part
↑
whole

8 → 3 ← part
  → 5 ← part
↑
whole

5 and 3 make 8   is the same as   3 and 5 make 8.

VOCABULARY: *altogether, whole, part*

MAKING EIGHT

What other numbers make 8? Look at the **number bonds** below.

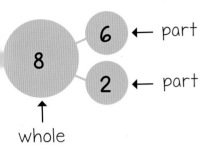 ← part
← part

whole

6 and 2 make 8.

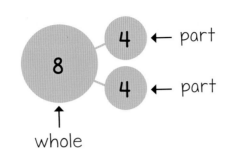 ← part
← part

whole

4 and 4 make 8.

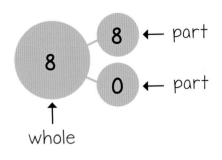 ← part
← part

whole

8 and 0 make 8.

TIME TO PRACTICE!

You can practice making number bonds using candies, small tomatoes, or grapes.

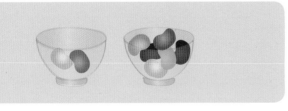

1 Count out eight candies.
Eight is the whole number of candies.

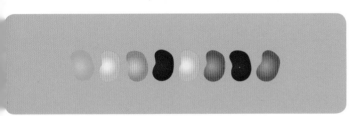

2 Split them into two groups, one group in each bowl. Each bowl holds part of the whole number of candies.

3 Pour the candies from both bowls onto the paper plate.

YOU WILL NEED:

- candies, small tomatoes, or grapes
- 2 small bowls
- a paper plate

4 Count the candies on the plate.
How many altogether?
The two parts together make the whole number.

5 Now divide the candies into the two bowls again and repeat.

PARENT AND TEACHER GUIDANCE

- Playing this game many times using different numbers in the original pile will strengthen children's understanding of the concept of whole and part numbers.

VOCABULARY: number bond

CREATING NUMBER BONDS

We can use cubes to show how number bonds work. Start with 5 cubes.

Make a number train of 5 cubes.

Then split the train into 3 cubes and 2 cubes.

How many cubes are there in each group?

Let's make a number bond to find the answer.

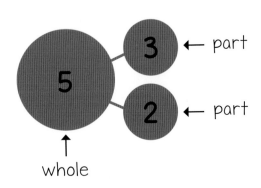

whole

What is the same in all the number bonds on this page? What is different?

3 and 2 make 5.

What other numbers make 5? Use your cubes to find out.

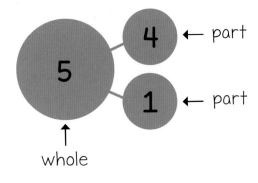

whole

4 and 1 make 5.

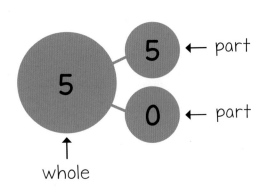

whole

5 and 0 make 5.

TRY THIS:

Imagine it is your birthday party. You have made 10 cups of juice. There are 4 cups of orange juice. The rest are all cranberry juice. How many cups contain cranberry juice?
Can you draw a number bond to show the answer for this game? ? stands for a missing number.

MISSING NUMBER

Look at the pictures below. ? stands for a missing number.
Can you figure out the missing number?
Look at all the triangles to see how the pattern works.

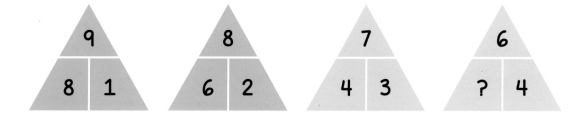

PARTY HATS

There are 8 cubes under these two party hats.
You can only lift one hat up.
Can you figure out how many cubes are under the other hat?
You can play this game at home. Hide cubes or toys under hats, boxes, or cups.

We can put numbers together to make greater numbers.

You have 3 crayons.

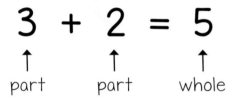

I give you 2 more crayons.

We use the word **add** to show that smaller numbers are joined together to make a greater number.

How many crayons do you have altogether?
Count all the crayons.
3 crayons and 2 more crayons make 5 crayons altogether.
We can write this as an **addition sentence**.

$$3 + 2 = 5$$

↑   ↑   ↑
part   part   whole

3 add 2 makes 5

We use the sign **+** to mean add or **plus**.
The sign **=** means is **equivalent** to, **equals**, or **make**.

ADDING BY COUNTING ON

We can add by **counting on**.

You have 9 and you add 1 more. Count on from 9.

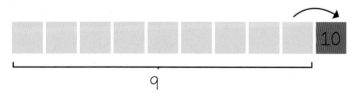

$$9 + 1 = 10$$

Nine plus one equals ten.
The answer is 10.

VOCABULARY: add, addition sentence, +, plus, =, equivalent, equals, make, counting on

COUNT THE APPLES

Practice counting on by counting the apples.

8 apples and 2 apples make ?

 and makes ?

Start at 8.
Count on 2 more.

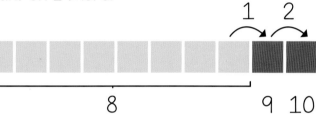

8 apples	and	2 apples	make	10 apples altogether.

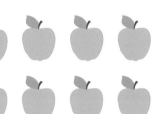 and  makes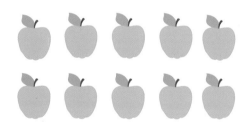

8	+	2	=	10
8	add	2	equals	10.

> ### PARENT AND TEACHER GUIDANCE
> - Show that the answer to an addition problem is the same whichever order you add the numbers.

TRY THIS:

Count on to find the answers to these additions.
Write an addition sentence for each one.

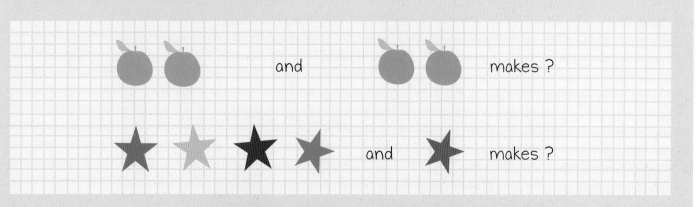

ADDING USING NUMBER BONDS

We can show addition sentences using number bonds too.

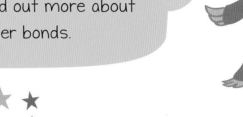
Look back at page 14 to find out more about number bonds.

Count the stars.

 add equals

7 + 3 = 10

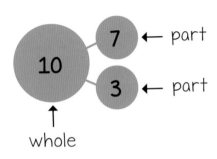

10

7 ← part

3 ← part

↑
whole

KITTEN COUNT

Practice using number bonds by adding the kittens and the toy mice.

How many kittens are there altogether?

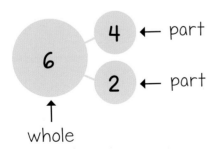

6

4 ← part

2 ← part

↑
whole

There are 6 kittens altogether.

How many toy mice are there altogether?

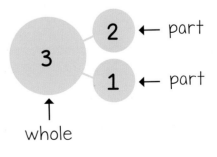

3

2 ← part

1 ← part

↑
whole

There are 3 toy mice altogether.

20

ADDITION PROBLEMS

Let's solve some addition problems.

It is Max's 7th birthday. All his friends have come to his birthday party. He receives 5 birthday presents. Then his cousins arrive with 2 more presents.

How many presents does Max have altogether?

Max has 7 presents altogether.

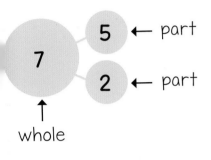

5 ← part

2 ← part

whole

$5 + 2 = 7$

4 people are in the roller coaster car. 2 more people get on. How many people will be in the roller coaster car altogether?

Write an addition sentence for this story. Draw a number bond.

There are 8 apples on the tree. There are 2 more on the ground.

Write an addition sentence for this story. Draw a number bond.

Make up some addition problems of your own! Draw pictures to show your problems.

We have learned to make greater numbers by adding.
Now let's make smaller numbers by **subtracting.**

Look back at page 11 to remind yourself about greater and smaller numbers.

I take 1 orange away from a group of 7 oranges.
There are 6 oranges left.
7 oranges with 1 taken away **leaves** 6.

When we write a **subtraction sentence**, we use the sign **–** to mean **minus** or **take away**.

$7 - 1 = 6$

Seven minus one equals six

We use the word minus to describe the part
that was taken away from the whole.

FLY AWAY BEES

Look at the bees and the flowers.

There are 6 bees.

2 fly away.
How many bees are left?

$6 - 2 = 4$

VOCABULARY: subtract, leaves, subtraction sentence, –, minus, take away

LESS THAN

Less than is another way of saying smaller than.

Can you say what 2 less than 5 is?
You need to subtract to find the answer.

5

3

5 – 2 = 3

What is 3 less than 8 cubes?
This is what it looks like.

8

5

8 – 3 = 5

Can you use marbles or cubes
to show 3 less than 9?

SUBTRACTING BY COUNTING ON

Counting on from the smaller number is another way to do subtraction.

5 – 3 = ?

Lay out 5 cubes.
Lay 3 cubes below the line of 5 cubes.
Look at the lines of cubes.
You can see the difference between 5 and 3.

How many will you have to count on from 3 to reach 5?

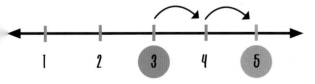

That's 1 step from 3 to 4, and 1 step from 4 to 5.
That's 2 steps altogether.

5 – 3 = 2

COUNTING BACK

Let's learn to subtract by
counting back.

9 – 2 = ?

Look at the number line.
To subtract by counting back you
have to start from the greater
number. The greater number in
this subtraction sentence is 9.

To subtract 2, you have to move
back 2 places along the number line.
You can draw arrows to show this.
The number you land on is the answer.

9 – 2 = 7

In a number line,
all the numbers are
arranged in order.

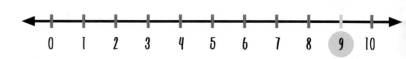

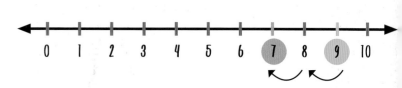

NUMBER BONDS

We can use number bonds to subtract.

There are 9 apples in a basket.
4 are red and the rest are green.
How many apples are green?

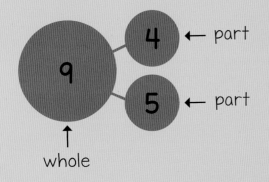

← part

← part

whole

There are five green apples.
9 – 4 = 5.

There are 10 cherries in a bowl.
If I eat 4, how many are left?

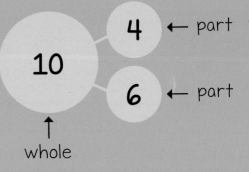

← part

← part

whole

There are 6 cherries left.
10 – 4 = 6.

SUBTRACTION PROBLEMS

Let's think about some subtraction problems.

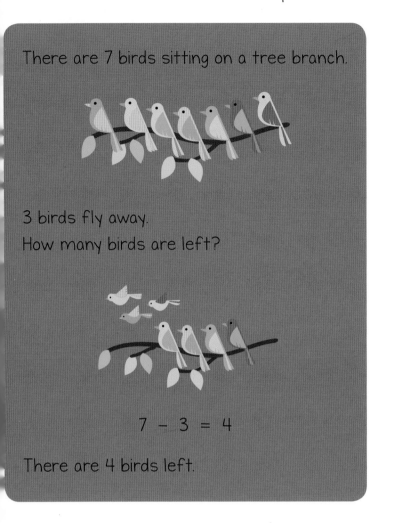

There are 7 birds sitting on a tree branch.

3 birds fly away.
How many birds are left?

7 – 3 = 4

There are 4 birds left.

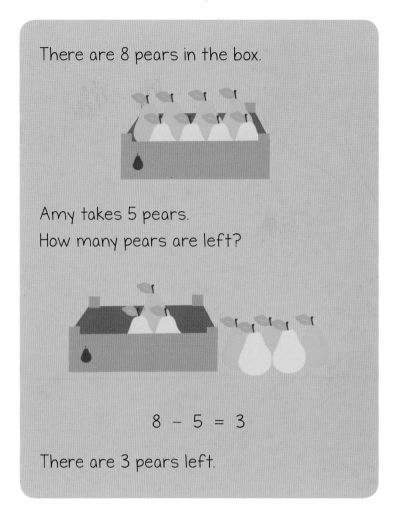

There are 8 pears in the box.

Amy takes 5 pears.
How many pears are left?

8 – 5 = 3

There are 3 pears left.

TRY THIS:

Look at these pictures and make up a subtraction problem.
Write a subtraction sentence to show your problem.

Make up some subtraction problems of your own!

25

Numbers that tell the **position** of something are called **ordinal numbers**.

The car that is **first** is the winner!

There are 5 cars in the race.

The red car is in first place.

The blue car is in **second** place.

The yellow car is in **third** place.

The black car is in **fourth** place.

The green car is in **fifth** place.

PARENT AND TEACHER GUIDANCE

- Use real-life examples to show the use of ordinal numbers and position words.
  Ask: "Which toy are you going to put in the box first?"
  "Who is third in the line?"
  "What piece of clothing will you put on second?"

Look at the children. They are waiting to jump on the trampoline.

| 1st | 2nd | 3rd | 4th | 5th | 6th | 7th | 8th | 9th | 10th |
| first | second | third | fourth | fifth | sixth | seventh | eighth | ninth | tenth |

Count along the ordinal numbers, pointing out which child is in which position.

Who is between the child in the brown t-shirt and the child wearing blue?

Who is before the child wearing red?

Who is after the child wearing white?

Who is **next to** the child wearing pink?

Who is **last** in the line?

You can look at the table to remember what you have learned about ordinal numbers.

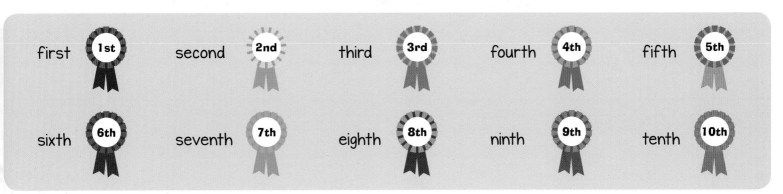

| first | 1st | second | 2nd | third | 3rd | fourth | 4th | fifth | 5th |
| sixth | 6th | seventh | 7th | eighth | 8th | ninth | 9th | tenth | 10th |

PARENT AND TEACHER GUIDANCE

● Make number cards 1 to 10. Ask children to lay them out in order, asking questions, such as, "Which card will come first?" "Which card comes second?"

VOCABULARY: sixth, seventh, eighth, ninth, tenth, next to, last

UNIT 6 NUMBERS TO 100

Let's learn about numbers that are greater than 10 and **place value**.

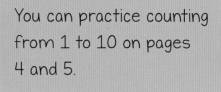

You can practice counting from 1 to 10 on pages 4 and 5.

Look at these numbers.

0 1 2 3 4 5 6 7 8 9

We need one **place** to write these numbers.
This is the **ones** place.

Now look at number 10.
We need two places to write this number.

Look at the boxes on the right.
The place on the right where 0 is written is the ones place.
The place on the left where 1 is written is the **tens** place.
The 0 in the ones place tells you that the number has 0 ones.
The 1 in the tens place tells you that the number has 1 ten.
Ten is made up of 1 ten and 0 ones.

tens place	ones place		
1	0	=	10

1 ten and 1 one make eleven.   = 11

1 ten and 2 ones make twelve.   = 12

1 ten and 3 ones make thirteen.   = 13

1 ten and 4 ones make fourteen.   = 14

1 ten and 5 ones make fifteen.   = 15

1 ten and 6 ones make sixteen.   = 16

1 ten and 7 ones make seventeen.   = 17

1 ten and 8 ones make eighteen.   = 18

1 ten and 9 ones make nineteen.   = 19

1 ten and 10 ones make twenty.   = 20

VOCABULARY: *place value, place, ones, tens*

COUNTING FORWARD AND BACKWARD

When you count forward, each number is one greater than the last number. Let's think about what happens when you count backward.

YOU WILL NEED:

- markers
- sticky notes in different colors
- a large sheet of paper
- cubes

1 Write numbers from 0 to 20 on sticky notes.

2 Arrange the sticky notes in the correct order on the large sheet of paper to make a **number track**.

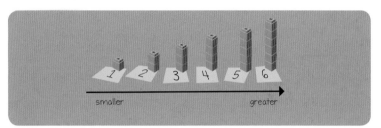

4 Count forward along the number track from 0 to 20. The numbers are getting greater as you count.

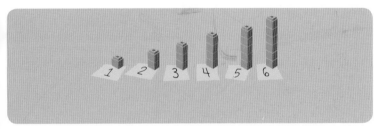

3 Place the right number of cubes on each sticky note.

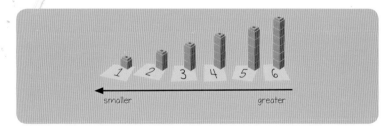

5 Count backward along the number track from 20 to 0. The numbers are getting smaller as you count.

PARENT AND TEACHER GUIDANCE

- Make a set of sticky notes with number names and practice matching names and numerals.

- Remove numbers from the track and ask, "Which number is missing?"

- Ask, "Tell me a number which is greater/smaller/one more than/one less than…"

VOCABULARY: number track

NUMBERS 21 AND BEYOND

Say the numbers and the number names aloud.

20	twenty	
21	twenty-one	
22	twenty-two	
23	twenty-three	
24	twenty-four	
25	twenty-five	
26	twenty-six	
27	twenty-seven	
28	twenty-eight	
29	twenty-nine	
30	thirty	
31	thirty-one	
32	thirty-two	

What do you think 33 looks like? Can you draw it?

40	forty	

What do you think 41 looks like? Can you draw it?

TRY THIS:

How many cherries can you see?

How many tens?
Which number will you write in the tens place?

How many ones?
Which number will you write in the ones place?

PARENT AND TEACHER GUIDANCE

- When children are fluent at counting numbers to 40, introduce numbers to 100. Talk about the words we use for larger numbers and how they are formed.

COUNTING IN TWOS

Let's learn to count in twos.

Count to 10 out loud.
When you count, you are adding 1 to get
to the next number each time.

How high can you count in ones?

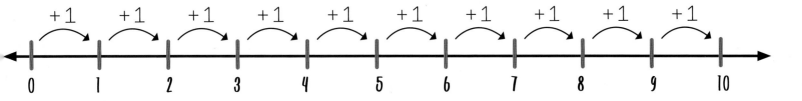

When you **skip count** in twos, you add 2 to get to the next number.
Count along the line, saying only the numbers that the arrow lands on.

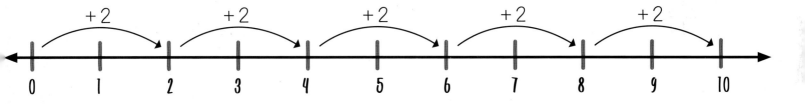

TRY THIS:

Take a handful of marbles.
Ask an adult to time how long it takes
for you to count them in ones.

Now count them in twos.
Is it quicker to count in ones or twos?

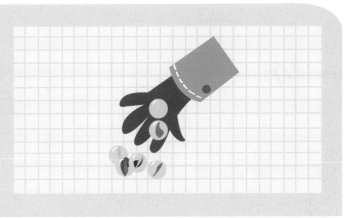

PARENT AND TEACHER GUIDANCE

- When children are fluent with numbers to 100, move on to skip counting in 5s and 10s to 100.

- Practice skip counting with items which are naturally in groups of 2, 5, or 10, such as shoes, gloves, and fingers.

- Once children have learned about money, practice skip counting with pennies, nickels, and dimes.

VOCABULARY: skip count

TOOLS FOR SUCCESS

Most of the math activities in the book can be carried out using everyday items, but the following mathematical tools are used in this book and you may find them useful.

Cubes

Cubes are perfect for teaching children counting, operations (addition, subtraction, multiplication, and division), place value, and early fractions. Sets of cubes that snap together are particularly useful.

Beads

Strings of beads can be used to recite number names in order from 0 to 20 or more, forward and backward. The color of beads can be varied every five beads to help children keep their place as they count.

Number line

A number line is a line with numbered points along it. A number line always has an arrow at each end to express the idea that it continues on infinitely. A number line can be used to count forward and backward, to count on or back in different sized steps, to help children find one more, one less, and so on, as well as for understanding the basics of addition and subtraction.

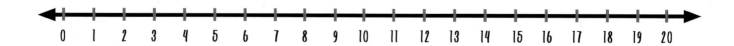

Number track

A number track shows numbers in order beginning at 1. Each space has a number in it and goes up in size order. These may be displayed on cards or on sticky notes or toys. A number track can be used in similar ways to a number line, but is particularly useful where numbers in the sequence can be masked or removed for finding missing numbers.

| 1 | 2 | 3 | 4 | 5 | 6 | 7 | 8 | 9 | 10 | 11 | 12 | 13 | 14 | 15 | 16 | 17 | 18 | 19 | 20 | 21 | 22 | 23 | 24 | 25 | 26 | 27 | 28 | 29 | 30 |

Ten-frame

A ten-frame is a two-by-five rectangular frame into which counters are placed to illustrate numbers less than or equal to ten. Several ten-frames together can show numbers larger than ten. Using ten-frames can help children develop their understanding of the number ten as well as its key position in our number system. In their simplest form, ten-frames can be drawn on paper, but you could also create a box with ten compartments, for example by adapting a large egg carton.